FIGHTING WITH LOVE

The Legacy of
JOHN LEWIS

Written by
Lesa Cline-Ransome

Illustrated by
James E. Ransome

A Paula Wiseman Book
SIMON & SCHUSTER BOOKS FOR YOUNG READERS
New York London Toronto Sydney New Delhi

SIMON & SCHUSTER BOOKS FOR YOUNG READERS • An imprint of Simon & Schuster Children's Publishing Division • 1230 Avenue of the Americas, New York, New York 10020 • Text © 2024 by Lesa Cline-Ransome • Illustration © 2024 by James E. Ransome • Book design by Laurent Linn © 2024 by Simon & Schuster, Inc. • All rights reserved, including the right of reproduction in whole or in part in any form. • SIMON & SCHUSTER BOOKS FOR YOUNG READERS and related marks are trademarks of Simon & Schuster, Inc. • Simon & Schuster: Celebrating 100 Years of Publishing in 2024 • For information about special discounts for bulk purchases, please contact Simon & Schuster Special Sales at 1-866-506-1949 or business@simonandschuster.com. • The Simon & Schuster Speakers Bureau can bring authors to your live event. For more information or to book an event, contact the Simon & Schuster Speakers Bureau at 1-866-248-3049 or visit our website at www.simonspeakers.com. • The text for this book was set in Caecilia LT Std. • The illustrations for this book were rendered using found, painted, and purchased papers with pencil drawing. • Manufactured in China • 1123 SCP • 10 9 8 7 6 5 4 3 2 • Library of Congress Cataloging-in-Publication Data • Names: Cline-Ransome, Lesa, author. | Ransome, James, illustrator. • Title: Fighting with love : the legacy of John Lewis / Lesa Cline-Ransome ; illustrated by James E. Ransome. • Other titles: Legacy of John Lewis • Description: First edition. | New York : Simon & Schuster Books for Young Readers, [2024] | "A Paula Wiseman Book." | Includes bibliographical references. | Audience: Ages 4–8 | Audience: Grades 2–3 | Summary: "In a beautiful prose telling, the story of a groundbreaking civil rights leader, John Lewis. John Lewis left a cotton farm in Alabama to join the fight for civil rights. He was only a teenager. He soon became a leader of a moment that changed a nation. Walking at the side of his mentor, Dr. Martin Luther King, Lewis was led by his belief in peaceful action and voting rights. Today and always his work and legacy will live on" —Provided by publisher. • Identifiers: LCCN 2022007298 (print) | LCCN 2022007299 (ebook) | ISBN 9781534496620 (hardcover) | ISBN 9781534496637 (ebook) • Subjects: LCSH: Lewis, John, 1940–2020—Juvenile literature. | African American civil rights workers—Biography—Juvenile literature. | Civil rights workers—United States—Biography—Juvenile literature. | African Americans—Civil rights—History—20th century—Juvenile literature. | United States—Race relations—Juvenile literature. • Classification: LCC E840.8.L43 C65 2023 (print) | LCC E840.8.L43 (ebook) | DDC 328.73/092 [B]—dc23/eng/20220328 • LC record available at https://lccn.loc.gov/2022007298 • LC ebook record available at https://lccn.loc.gov/2022007299

In memory of my dear friend Lisa Reticker.
Her fighting spirit lives on.
—L. C.-R.

To my friend Jerry Pinkney
(December 22, 1939–October 20, 2021).
Thanks for the time.
—J. E. R.

Before John Robert Lewis was old enough to read the word "love" in his Bible, he could feel it all around him. Not in the sun-beaten, sweat-soaked, hunchbacked farming his family did day in and day out. But in the clucking of chickens in the coop out in back of his home; in tending the garden bursting with butter beans, turnips, collards, and peppers; sitting in the pews at the Macedonia Baptist church; and surrounded by his momma, Willie Mae, his daddy, Eddie, and his nine brothers and sisters.

Love followed John just about everywhere he went, except on Saturday mornings when he and his daddy drove their mule and wagon into downtown Troy, Alabama.

Outside Byrd's Drugs, John hated that he and his daddy had to eat standing up outdoors instead of sitting down inside at the Whites Only lunch counter. And if the day was hot and dusty, John hated quenching his thirst at the rusty water spigot instead of at the shiny Whites Only fountain. Election day meant Whites Only could pick the laws, mayors, and presidents. John hated that colored folks had to stick to picking cotton.

In the fields, marching up one row and down another, John plowed and planted, chopped and picked alongside his family. One, two, three, four hundred pounds of cotton each day till their hands were bloodied. Insects, drought, low cotton prices, the white men's math that never added up to enough, all kept John's family working harder and longer, season after season.

"Working for nothing," is what John mumbled to his parents as he dragged his cotton sack behind him.

"God's gonna take care of his children," his momma told him, and kept on, picking all day, praying all night.

During harvest time, when his extra hands were needed on the farm, the school bus bumped along past John's house, leaving him behind.

After the workday was done, John read all he had—the Sears, Roebuck and Co. catalog, old copies of the *Montgomery Advertiser* newspaper, and his Bible—to keep up with his schooling.

On the days he wanted more, John hid under his porch and hopped onto the bus that would take him to school instead of to the fields.

The way John saw it, Troy was two separate towns. One for white folks, with paved roads, a library, new schools, and brand-new playgrounds. The other for colored people, with hand-me-down desks, donated school supplies, and muddy roads, for buses so likely to break down that students could board in the morning and not get to school until lunchtime.

One Sunday morning, as the Lewis family tuned in to the scratchy WRMA station out of Montgomery, John heard a young preacher named Martin Luther King Jr. through the radio speakers.

"Take a stand for truth and justice," the young preacher said. "Sometimes it might mean going to jail."

Fifteen years of Sunday service, and this was the first time John had heard the words "justice" and "segregation" from a pulpit. John listened quietly, but his heart was shouting "Amen."

"Don't get in trouble," John's mother fussed when he left for the Greyhound bus terminal on his way to the American Baptist Theological Seminary in Nashville, Tennessee. But they both knew that as long as you were a Negro in the segregated South, getting in trouble wouldn't be hard to do. Whether you were riding a bus in Montgomery, attending a high school in Little Rock, Arkansas, or greeting a white woman at a grocery store in Money, Mississippi, trouble would always be waiting.

John had decided on the very Sunday morning when he'd heard the young preacher on the radio that he too would take a stand for what he believed. When Reverend King led the Montgomery bus boycott and used his pulpit to demand that Negroes should be able to sit where they pleased and not only in the backs of buses, John saw that the gospel could change not just hearts but laws, too.

John knew that standing up to segregation would mean hard work, but he also knew what years of marching up and down rows of cotton fields had taught him—that hard work meant long days and longer nights. So, after washing dishes in the school cafeteria to pay his tuition, studying late into the night, and practicing his sermons, John started marching.

Right away, he joined the Nashville chapter of the National Association for the Advancement of Colored People, nicknamed the NAACP. And every Tuesday, in the basement of Clark Memorial United Methodist Church, John listened to the words "love" and "peace," "justice" and "nonviolence" from Pastor James Lawson, a friend of Reverend Martin Luther King. John knew scripture from his own Bible, but now he learned about love in the holy books of Judaism, Islam, Buddhism, and Hinduism, and in the teachings of a man named Mahatma Gandhi.

No matter how hateful the action, John grew to believe, "No child is born in hate."

At first there were just John, Diane Nash, Paul LaPrad, Marion Barry, and several other students. Empty chairs filled the meeting room. But word spread. John brought his roommate Bernard Lafayette, and soon the empty chairs were filled.

United by their love of human and civil rights, John and other college students gathered at the Highlander Folk School. They planned how to end segregation through nonviolent protest, just like students were already doing with their lunch counter sit-ins in Greensboro, North Carolina. For John, fighting with his heart was his most powerful tool. "Nonviolence is love in action," he said.

They took turns playing the part of the angry whites they would face, and acted out standing silently while being shouted and cursed at. They practiced how to curl in tight on the ground to protect themselves from kicks and punches that would beat down on them. They remembered to look into the eyes of their attackers, reminding them that a child of God was looking back.

After hearing the words and feeling the fists, some never finished their training at Highlander, leaving as fast as they'd come, asking what kind of love means you've got to be beaten up outside and in.

But John knew. "It is a love that accepts and embraces the hateful and the hurtful." And so, John stayed and practiced some more.

John and his group began their protest at Harvey's Department Store in downtown Nashville. The first step was to make sure each store and movie theater in town was denying Negroes service. The next step was to make sure everyone in the country knew it. The last step would be to demand that it end.

Dressed in their Sunday best, John's group came in and took seats near the white customers at the lunch counter.

"It is our policy not to serve colored people here," the manager had told them a couple months earlier when they tried to place an order. Now they were back. They sat as still as stone.

All their months of training had prepared them for this very moment.

The students spread out over the city staging sit-ins and returned again and again. COUNTER CLOSED signs were slammed down in front of them. Employees turned the lights off in stores. Locked the students out and locked them in. But the protestors kept coming back. To Woolworth's, to W. T. Grant's, to Kress's, to Walgreen's, to McClellan's, all over Nashville. Each time to larger, angrier groups of whites who shouted and cursed, kicked and punched.

Each time, more crowds gathered, news cameras filmed, reporters wrote articles, and people across the country began paying attention. The police watched too, but not one stepped in to help the students. Finally the police came forward with handcuffs.

"Disorderly conduct," the police shouted as they arrested the orderly protesters and led them away in paddy wagons.

"We're here so that people will love each other," John told the officers as the protestors were packed inside and carted off to jail. Side by side in their jail cells, they refused bail, prayed, sang songs. "It was like deliverance," John said, rejoicing as if he were back in church on Sunday morning.

"You can get hurt," his mother worried. "You can get killed."

"When you see something that's not right . . . you have to do something," he told her.

After a bomb attack destroyed the home of a lawyer helping them, John and five thousand others marched up streets and down to Nashville city hall, demanding action and a response from the mayor.

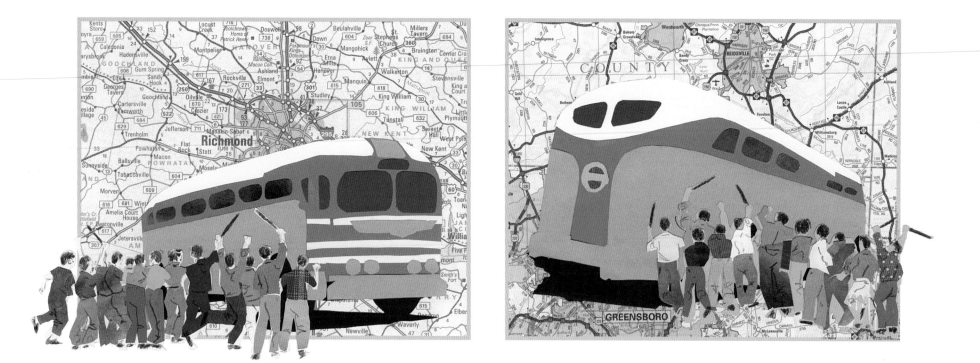

With the world watching, he answered. The mayor appealed to Nashville citizens to "end discrimination, to have no bigotry, no bias, no hatred." All of those words meant no more segregation in the city of Nashville.

Winning one city meant others in the South could be won too. John missed his graduation because he was marching onto a Greyhound bus as one of hundreds of Freedom Riders, white and Negro protesters traveling together throughout the South during the summer of 1961. Atlanta and Anniston. Richmond and Rock Hill. Petersburg and New Orleans. Riding to desegregate buses and waiting rooms. At nearly every stop they were met by white mobs, barking police and their dogs, bomb threats, and angry chants.

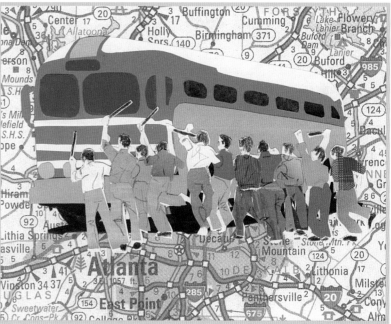

Stop singing and start fighting, some folks told John. *Why are Negroes the only ones going to funerals?* others asked, after homes and churches were bombed. Bandaged and bruised, the Freedom Riders again climbed aboard.

John marched with hundreds of thousands of people up to Washington, DC, at the March on Washington, where he stood tall with other civil rights giants in front of the Lincoln Memorial. "We march today for jobs and freedom," John preached into the microphone. "We want our freedom and we want it now."

As John's voice and the nonviolent movement grew stronger, segregation grew weaker. He watched as President Kennedy worked with protest leaders to create a civil rights bill in 1963. After Kennedy's death, it was President Lyndon Johnson who signed the Civil Rights Act of 1964 into law, protecting all citizens from discrimination based on race. He also witnessed President Johnson signing the Voting Rights Act of 1965, which made it illegal to make it harder for people of color to vote.

These laws came from the hard work of Lewis and his fellow Freedom Riders and protesters. They marched and fought to remind the world that Negroes would never forget they were equal citizens in the eyes of God and the law.

John led a march that began in Selma, Alabama. Standing at the foot of the Edmund Pettus Bridge in Selma, he was ready. John had stood up for teachers and farmers, students and servants, for everyone who needed someone to stand up for what was right, and he was ready again to keep standing up.

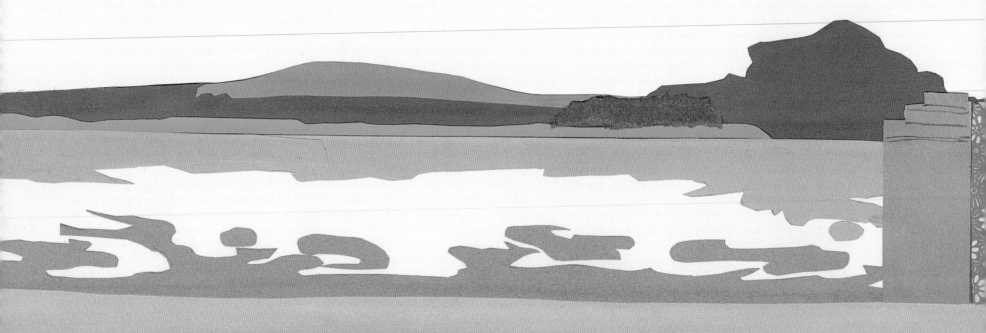

"Hold only love, only peace in your heart, knowing that the battle of good to overcome evil is already won," John said.

Not one hundred miles from the fields in Troy where he'd plowed and planted, chopped and picked as a boy, John looked across at a wall of police officers, some on horses blocking the marchers' way.

"God's gonna take care of his children," his mother had told him.
He bowed his head and prayed.

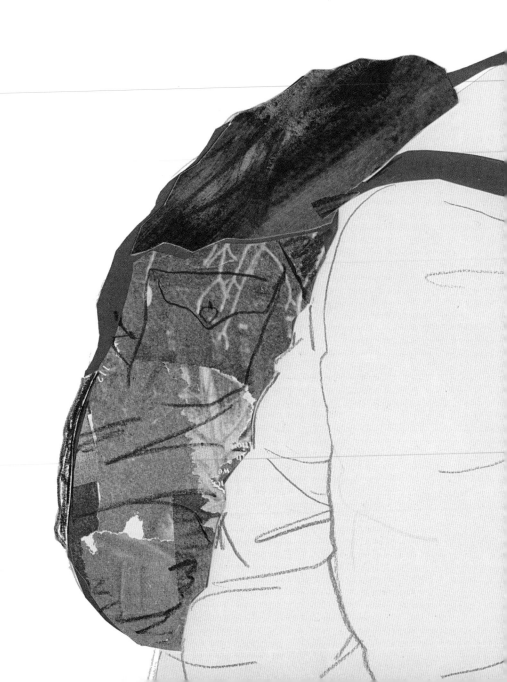

John locked arms with those beside him and began marching up, down,

and forward.

John Lewis on the Edmund Pettus Bridge in Selma, Alabama, in 2015, fifty years after he led an attempted march over the bridge from Selma to Montgomery, Alabama.

If not us, then who? If not now, then when?
—John Lewis

On Sunday, March 7, 1965, twenty-five-year-old John Lewis and fellow civil rights activist Hosea Williams led a group of six hundred protesters across the Edmund Pettus Bridge in Selma, Alabama. The march was intended to proceed fifty-four miles down Route 80 to the state capital of Montgomery and the office of Governor George Wallace to demand voting rights for Negro citizens. However, before they could cross the bridge, they were met with mounted state troopers, who sprayed them with tear gas and rubber bullets and beat them with billy clubs. Fifty-eight people were hospitalized, including Lewis, whose skull was cracked. He later recalled thinking in the moment, "I'm going to die here."

The march came to be known as "Bloody Sunday" and helped lead to the passage of the Voting Rights Act of 1965.

Two weeks after "Bloody Sunday," Reverends Martin Luther King Jr. and Ralph Abernathy returned to the bridge and led another march under the protection of federal troops.

Born near Troy, Alabama, on February 21, 1940, John Lewis was fifteen years old when the landmark *Brown v. Board of Education* decision was handed down by the US Supreme Court, declaring that separate but equal schools were illegal. A congressman from Mississippi referred to the day of that ruling as "Black Monday." Officials in Lewis's home state of Alabama chose to ignore the laws requiring schools to desegregate. One year and three months after that decision, a fourteen-year-old boy named Emmett Till, from Chicago, visiting relatives in Money, Mississippi, entered a store where a white woman named Carolyn Bryant was working behind the counter. She claimed Till "offended" her and told her husband, Roy. Bryant and several of his relatives forcibly took Till from his uncle's home later that evening, murdered him, and threw his maimed body in the Tallahatchie River, only to be discovered days later. Roy Bryant and his brother, J. W. Milam, were acquitted of all charges stemming from the murder of Emmett Till by an all-white jury. Three months later, the Montgomery bus boycott began.

These momentous events in Lewis's formative years motivated his lifelong quest to change a system of injustice, corruption, inequality, and discrimination.

Arrested forty-five times during protests, including several while serving as a member of Congress, Lewis even served a brief sentence at the infamous Parchman Farm penitentiary in Mississippi, yet he continued his fight for equality throughout his life and career.

He served as chairman of the Student Nonviolent Coordinating Committee (SNCC), was one of the thirteen original Freedom Riders, was elected to the Atlanta City Council, and became a United States congressman representing Georgia's fifth district in 1986. He served seventeen consecutive terms.

John Lewis was called "the conscience of Congress" by House Speaker Nancy Pelosi, and *Time* magazine named him on its list of "messengers of love and hope."

He is considered one of the Big Six leaders of the civil rights movement.

In 2011, President Barack Obama awarded him the Presidential Medal of Freedom, the nation's highest civilian honor.

Relentless, inspiring, undaunted, John Lewis was my hero. One of my greatest honors was meeting him in 2017 while attending a Black American Library Association event in Atlanta, Georgia. He was in person just as I imagined he would be—a gracious gentleman with a quick laugh.

Gone, but not forgotten, he and his loving legacy remind us all to keep marching.

The author, Lesa Cline-Ransome, and illustrator, James Ransome, with John Lewis
at the Tenth National Conference of African American Librarians in Atlanta.

Get in good trouble, necessary trouble, and help redeem the soul of America.
—*John Lewis*

February 21, 1940: John Lewis is born, the third of ten children, to Willie Mae and Eddie Lewis near Troy, Alabama.

1945: Lewis begins reading the family Bible and starts ministering to chickens on the family farm to practice preaching sermons.

1951: At eleven years old, Lewis travels north for the first time to visit family in Buffalo, New York, and experiences integration in action. "It was another world," Lewis recalled.

May 17, 1954: The US Supreme Court hands down its unanimous ruling in the *Brown v. Board of Education* case, ruling that it is illegal to separate children in public schools because of their race.

August–September 1955: Fourteen-year-old Emmett Till is murdered in Money, Mississippi, for speaking to a white woman. His open-casket funeral and the trial of his murderers make national headlines. Lewis, fifteen years old at the time, remembered, "I was fifteen, Black. . . . He could have been me."

1956: Lewis hears a Martin Luther King Jr. sermon on the radio and is introduced to nonviolent religious protest. "From that moment on, I decided I wanted to be just like him," Lewis said.

Fall 1957: Lewis is accepted as a student at the American Baptist Theological Seminary and plans to leave home to attend school in Nashville, Tennessee.

September 4, 1957: Nine Black students enroll at all white Central High School in Little Rock, Arkansas, and are met with the Arkansas National Guard to block their entry. President Dwight D. Eisenhower sends in federal troops on September 25 to safely escort them to class, prompting a wave of national media coverage.

Fall 1957: In response to the "Little Rock Nine" students, Lewis decides to desegregate Troy State University. On Christmas Day, he writes to MLK for advice. He is invited to meet with him in Montgomery the following summer. MLK tells him, "If you really want to do it, we will see you through." Because of safety concerns, his parents convince him to abandon his efforts.

Fall 1958: Lewis begins attending nonviolence workshops organized by Reverend James Morris Lawson Jr. "It changed my life forever, set me on a path, committed to the way of peace, to the way of love, and I have not looked back since," Lewis said.

1960–1961: In 1960, Lewis is arrested for the first of over forty times during a sit-in at a lunch counter. His many arrests in the struggle for civil rights occur at sit-ins, mass meetings, and the landmark "Freedom Rides" of 1961 that test racial segregation in the South.

August 28, 1963: John is a featured speaker at the March on Washington for Jobs and Freedom with MLK as he delivers his now famous "I Have a Dream" speech. As Student Nonviolent Coordinating Committee (SNCC) chairperson, John also delivers prepared remarks. "We do not want to go to jail, but we will go to jail if this is the price we must pay for love, brotherhood, and true peace," he says.

September 15, 1963: Lewis is back home when he receives news that four young girls have been killed at Sixteenth Street Baptist Church in a bombing in Birmingham. He departs for Birmingham immediately to coordinate support for community members.

November 22, 1963: President John F. Kennedy is assassinated in Dallas, Texas. "He represented our hope, our idealism, our dreams about what America could become. . . ." Lewis said. "When he died, a light went out in America and the nation has never quite been the same since."

March 7, 1965: Lewis is one of six hundred voting rights marchers who are met with Alabama State Troopers as they cross the Edmund Pettus Bridge from Selma to Montgomery in a violent confrontation now known as "Bloody Sunday." Lewis is hospitalized for two days because of the injuries he sustains. "Selma, the bridge, was a test of the belief that love was stronger than hate," Lewis said. "And it is. Much stronger. So much stronger."

April 4, 1968: Martin Luther King Jr. is assassinated. "From the time I was fifteen until the day he died . . . he was the person who, more than any other, continued to influence my life, who made me who I was," Lewis said. "He made me who I am."

1971: Lewis becomes executive director of the Voter Education Project, a program of the Southern Regional Council.

April 5, 1977: In his first bid for Congress in metro Atlanta, Lewis loses in a runoff. Later that year, President Jimmy Carter appoints him to direct ACTION, a federal volunteer agency.

October 6, 1981: Lewis wins his election for his seat on the Atlanta City Council, his first political office. He serves until 1986.

November 4, 1986: After a heated primary, Lewis wins a congressional seat with support from fellow activist and Atlanta mayor Andrew Young. He is elected to Congress representing Georgia's fifth district, which includes much of Atlanta. He goes on to be re-elected sixteen times, only once receiving less than 70 percent of the vote.

2001: Lewis receives the John F. Kennedy Profile in Courage Award for Lifetime Achievement. "Courage is not rooted in reason but rather courage comes from a divine purpose to make things right," Lewis states during his acceptance speech.

April 27, 2009: In Washington during a demonstration at the embassy of Sudan, Lewis and four others are arrested. The demonstration is to protest the expulsion of aid workers amid a humanitarian crisis.

February 15, 2011: In the East Room of the White House, Lewis is presented with the Presidential Medal of Freedom, the nation's highest civilian honor, by President Barack Obama.

March 7, 2015: Lewis joins President Obama, former president George W. Bush, and thousands of others in Selma at the commemoration of the fiftieth anniversary of Bloody Sunday. President Obama says of Lewis and his fellow marchers, "Our job's easier because somebody already got us through that first mile. Somebody already got us over that bridge."

June 22, 2016: To protest a lack of action on gun control measures, Lewis leads a Democratic sit-in on the House floor.

July 17, 2020: Lewis dies at the age of eighty. In an essay sent to the *Atlanta Journal-Constitution* two days before his death, he writes, "Though I may not be here with you, I urge you to answer the highest calling of your heart and stand up for what you truly believe. In my life I have done all I can to demonstrate that the way of peace, the way of love and nonviolence is the more excellent way. Now it is your turn to let freedom ring."

"In the fields . . ."

"Working for nothing": John Lewis with Michael D'Orso, *Walking with the Wind*, p. 11.

"God's gonna take care of his children": John Lewis with Michael D'Orso, *Walking with the Wind*, p. 14.

"One Sunday morning . . ."

"Take a stand for truth and justice. . . . Sometimes it might mean going to jail": Jon Meacham, *His Truth Is Marching On*, p. 34.

"Don't get in trouble . . ."

"Don't get in trouble": TED Legacy Project video, 4:58.

"Right away he joined . . ."

"No child is born in hate": Jon Meacham, *His Truth Is Marching On*, p. 91.

"United by their love . . ."

"Nonviolence is love in action": John Lewis with Michael D'Orso, *Walking with the Wind*, p. 189.

"They took turns playing . . ."

"It is a love that accepts and embraces the hateful and the hurtful": John Lewis with Michael D'Orso, *Walking with the Wind*, p. 77.

"John and his group . . ."

"It is our policy not to serve colored people here": John Lewis with Michael D'Orso, *Walking with the Wind*, p. 88.

"Each time, more crowds gathered . . ."

"Disorderly conduct": John Lewis with Michael D'Orso, *Walking with the Wind*, p. 100.

"We're here so that people will love each other": Jon Meacham, *His Truth Is Marching On*, p. 91.

"It was like deliverance": John Lewis with Michael D'Orso, *Walking with the Wind*, p. 101.

"You can get hurt . . ."

"You can get hurt. You can get killed": TED Legacy Project video, 5:01.

"When you see something that's not right . . . you have to do something": TED Legacy Project video, 0:16.

"end discrimination, to have no bigotry, no bias, no hatred": John Lewis with Michael D'Orso, *Walking with the Wind*, p. 110.

"John marched with hundreds of thousands . . ."

"We march today for jobs and freedom. We want our freedom and we want it now": John Lewis with Michael D'Orso, *Walking with the Wind*, pp. 219–220.

"Hold only love, only peace . . ."

"Hold only love, only peace in your heart, knowing that the battle of good to overcome evil is already won": John Lewis with Brenda Jones, *Across That Bridge*, p. 178.

Author's Note

"I'm going to die here": Jon Meacham, *His Truth Is Marching On*, p. 197.

Time Line

"Speak up, speak out, get in the way. Get in good trouble, necessary trouble, and help redeem the soul of America": Associated Press, "From Rep. John Lewis, Quotes in a Long Life of Activism," July 18, 2020.

"It was another world": Jon Meacham, *His Truth Is Marching On*, p. 30.

"I was fifteen, Black. . . . He could have been me": Jon Meacham, *His Truth Is Marching On*, p. 38.

"From that moment on, I decided I wanted to be just like him": Jon Meacham, *His Truth Is Marching On*, p. 35.

"If you really want to do it, we will see you through": Jon Meacham, *His Truth Is Marching On*, p. 51.

"It changed my life forever, set me on a path, committed to the way of peace, to the way of love, and I have not looked back since": Jon Meacham, *His Truth Is Marching On*, p. 58.

"We do not want to go to jail, but we will go to jail if this is the price we must pay for love, brotherhood, and true peace": Jon Meacham, *His Truth Is Marching On*, p. 141.

"He represented our hope, our idealism, our dreams about what America could become. . . . When he died, a light went out in America and the nation has never quite been the same since": Jon Meacham, *His Truth Is Marching On*, p. 153.

"Selma, the bridge, was a test of the belief that love was stronger than hate. And it is. Much stronger. So much stronger": Jon Meacham, *His Truth Is Marching On*, p. 185.

"From the time I was fifteen until the day he died . . . he was the person who, more than any other, continued to influence my life, who made me who I was. He made me who I am": John Lewis with Michael D'Orso, *Walking with the Wind*, p. 412.

"Courage is not rooted in reason but rather courage comes from a divine purpose to make things right": John Lewis, acceptance speech upon receiving the John F. Kennedy Profile in Courage Award for Lifetime Achievement, May 21, 2001, John F. Kennedy Library and Museum, Boston.

"Our job's easier because somebody already got us through that first mile. Somebody already got us over that bridge": Barack Obama, "Remarks by the President at the Fiftieth Anniversary of the Selma to Montgomery Marches," March 7, 2015, Edmund Pettus Bridge, Selma, AL.

"Though I may not be here with you, I urge you to answer the highest calling of your heart and stand up for what you truly believe. In my life I have done all I can to demonstrate that the way of peace, the way of love and nonviolence is the more excellent way. Now it is your turn to let freedom ring": John Lewis, "Together, You Can Redeem the Soul of Our Nation," July 30, 2020, *New York Times*.

Lewis, John, with Brenda Jones. *Across That Bridge: Life Lessons and a Vision for Change*. New York: Hyperion, 2012.

Lewis, John, with Michael D'Orso. *Walking with the Wind: A Memoir of the Movement*. New York: Simon & Schuster, 1998.

Meacham, Jon. *His Truth Is Marching On: John Lewis and the Power of Hope*. New York: Random House, 2020.

TED Legacy Project. "John Lewis and Bryan Stevenson: The Fight for Civil Rights and Freedom." TED video. November 19, 2019.